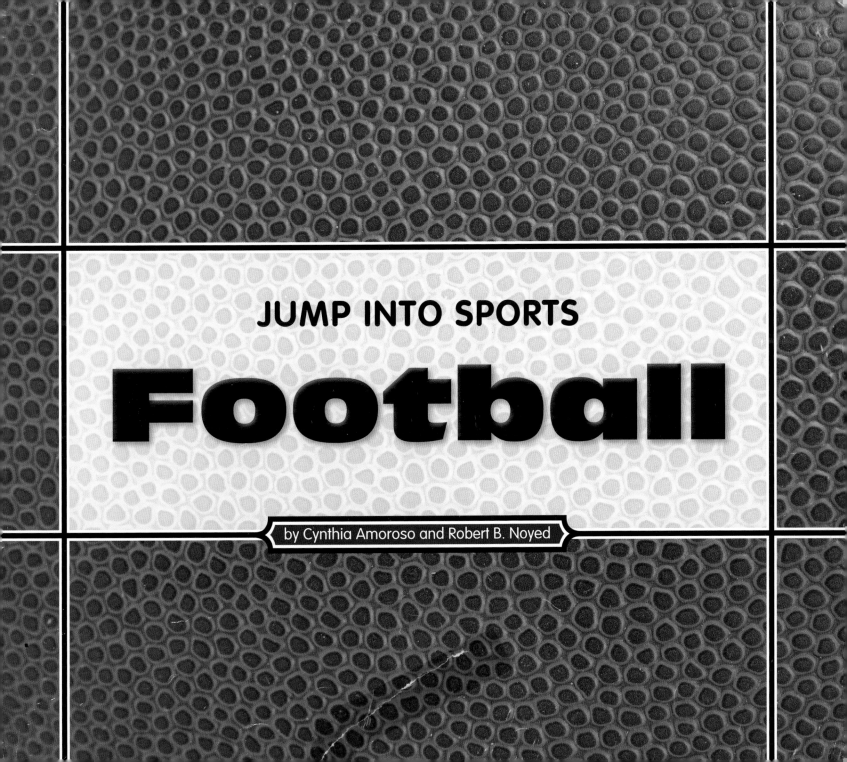

JUMP INTO SPORTS

Football

by Cynthia Amoroso and Robert B. Noyed

Get your **equipment**!
It is time to play
football.

Football is played with an oval-shaped ball with pointed ends.

Football is played on a large field. The field is 100 yards long.

Many football games are played in large **stadiums** so fans can watch.

Players wear helmets on their heads. A mask on the helmet protects the player's face. Players also wear pads on their shoulders, knees, and hips.

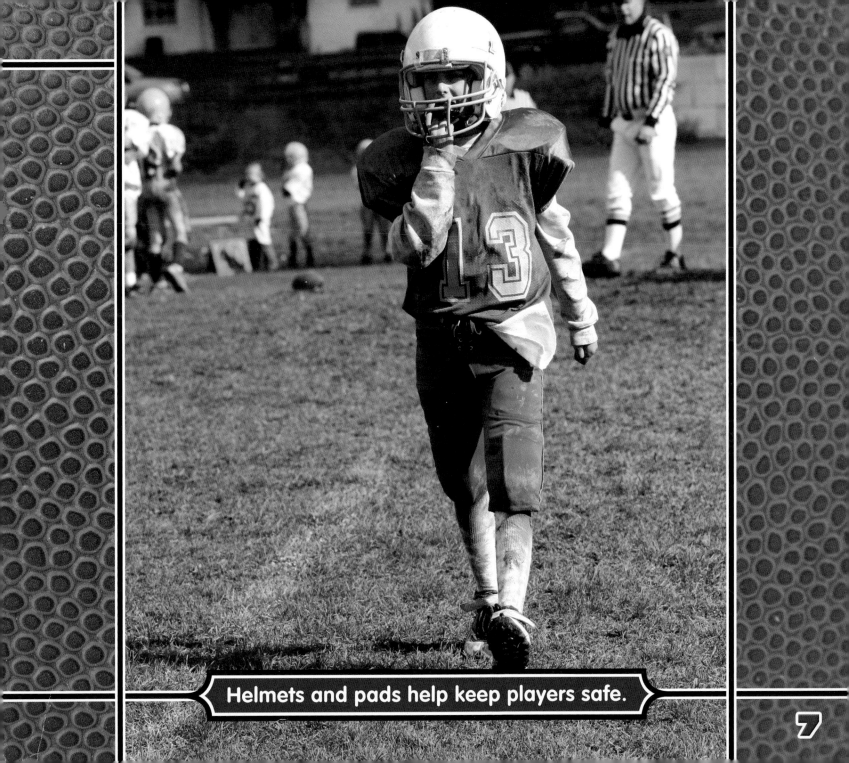

Helmets and pads help keep players safe.

In a game, each team has 11 players on the field. The team with the ball is called the **offense**. The team without the ball is the **defense**.

There is a lot of **contact** in football.

The offense tries to get the ball to the **end zone**. If they do, it is called a **touchdown**. They get six points.

The player with the ball runs quickly to the end zone.

Every player on the offense has a job. Some players block. They keep the other team from getting to the person with the ball. Players on offense can also pass, catch, or run with the ball.

The **quarterback** often throws the football to his teammates.

The defense tries to keep the offense from scoring. They try to **tackle** the player who has the ball.

Football players train to be strong enough to tackle other players.

Each play is called a **down**. The team on offense tries to gain 10 yards in four downs. If the team on defense stops them, the defense gets the ball. Then it is their turn to play offense.

Football players line up against each other at the start of each down.

In some football games, players do not tackle. Instead, they grab a flag from the ball carrier's waist to stop them. This is called flag football.

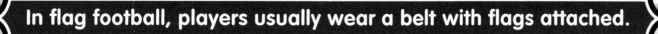
In flag football, players usually wear a belt with flags attached.

However you play, football
is a great game!

Football is a fun game to play with friends!

Glossary

contact (KON-takt): Contact means touching. There is a lot of contact when football players tackle each other.

defense (DEE-fenss): The defense is the players who are trying to stop the other team from scoring. Players on defense try to tackle the player who has the ball.

down (DOWN): A down is a chance for the offense to advance the football. The offense has four chances to move the ball 10 yards forward.

end zone (END zohn): An end zone is the area at the end of the football field. A team must get the football to the end zone to score.

equipment (ih-KWIP-munt): Equipment are the things used to play a sport. Football equipment includes helmets and footballs.

offense (AW-fenss): The offense is the players who are trying to score. The offense makes plays to move toward the end zone.

quarterback (KWOR-tur-bak): The quarterback is the player who leads the offense. The quarterback often passes or hands off the football.

stadiums (STAY-dee-uhmz): Stadiums are large arenas where people can watch sports teams. Many stadiums can hold thousands of people.

tackle (TAK-ull): To tackle is to knock a person to the ground. In football, players tackle the other team to stop them from scoring.

touchdown (TUCH-down): A touchdown is when a team gets the football into the end zone. A touchdown is worth six points.

To Find Out More

Books

Gibbons, Gail. *My Football Book*. New York: HarperCollins, 2000.

Kalman, Bobbie, and John Crossingham. *Huddle Up Football*. New York: Crabtree Publishing Company, 2007.

Savage, Jeff. *Play-By-Play Football*. Minneapolis, MN: Lerner, 2003.

Wingate, Brian. *Football: Rules, Tips, Strategy, and Safety*. New York: Rosen Publishing Group, 2007.

Web Sites

Visit our Web site for links about football: *childsworld.com/links*

Note to Parents, Teachers, and Librarians: We routinely verify our Web links to make sure they are safe and active sites. So encourage your readers to check them out!

Index

About the Authors

Cynthia Amoroso has worked as an elementary school teacher and a high school English teacher. Writing children's books is another way for her to share her passion for the written word.

Robert B. Noyed has worked as a newspaper reporter and in the communications department for a Minnesota school district. He enjoys the challenge and accomplishment of writing children's books.

On the cover: Football is often played in the fall.

Published by The Child's World®
1980 Lookout Drive • Mankato, MN 56003-1705
800-599-READ • www.childsworld.com

ACKNOWLEDGMENTS
The Child's World®: Mary Berendes, Publishing Director
The Design Lab: Design and production
Red Line Editorial: Editorial direction

PHOTO CREDITS: Jacom Stephens/iStockphoto, cover; Nick M. Do/
iStockphoto, cover; PhotoDisc, 2; Miroslav Ferkuniak/iStockphoto,
3; Big Stock Photo, 5, 9, 13; Amy Meyers/Shutterstock Images, 7, 11;
Daniel Padavona/iStockphoto, 15; Jane Norton/iStockphoto, 17; Kris
Hanke/iStockphoto, 19; iStockphoto, 21

Printed in the United States of America in Mankato, Minnesota.
November 2009
F11460

LIBRARY OF CONGRESS CATALOGING-IN-PUBLICATION DATA
Amoroso, Cynthia.
  Football / by Cynthia Amoroso and Robert B. Noyed.
    p. cm. — (Jump into sports)
  Includes bibliographical references and index.
  ISBN 978-1-60253-369-1 (library bound : alk. paper)
  1. Football—Juvenile literature. I. Noyed, Robert B. II. Title. III. Series.
  GV950.7.A56 2009
  796.33—dc22   2009030727

All sports carry a certain amount of risk. To reduce the risk of injury while playing football, play at your own level, wear all safety gear, and use care and common sense. The publisher and author take no responsibility or liability for injuries resulting from playing football.